HISTORY OF THE WINDMILL

Windmills have been used for hundreds of years. Windmills have long been associated with the country of Holland, but they weren't built there until the late 1500s.

The first written record of ancient windmills was recorded in Persia between 500-900 AD. The Chinese were also using windmills as early as 1219 AD although some historians believe they may have had the technology much earlier, around 200 BC.

THE POWER OF THE WIND HARVESTED

Understanding Wind Power for Kids | Children's Electricity Books

Speedy Publishing LLC

40 E. Main St. #1156

Newark, DE 19711

www.speedypublishing.com

Copyright 2018

All Rights reserved. No part of this book may be reproduced or used in any way or form or by any means whether electronic or mechanical, this means that you cannot record or photocopy any material ideas or tips that are provided in this book.

In this book, we're going to talk about how wind power is harvested. So, let's get right to it!

These ancient windmills were blades that sat on the top of a building or tower. The power of the wind turned the blades.

In ancient times, this power was used primarily for pumping water or for grinding grain to make flour. Windmills weren't used to create electricity yet.

WINDMILL IN BURGUNDY, FRANCE

Windmill designs continued to be improved as the centuries passed. Throughout the 1700s in Europe, millwrights, who were builders specializing in windmill design, continued to revise and improve them.

Their goal was to get as much energy as possible from wind power so that water could be pumped faster and grinding grain into flour would be a faster process. In the 1800s, these dramatic improvements in windmill design meant that windmills became powerful enough to generate the power needed for sawmills.

SAWMILL

In the sawmills, huge saws were used to cut through the trunks of thick trees to create the necessary lumber needed for building.

TOBACCO FARM

In addition to powering sawmills, windmills were also used for the processing of tobacco and various dyes, as well as for the grinding of spices.

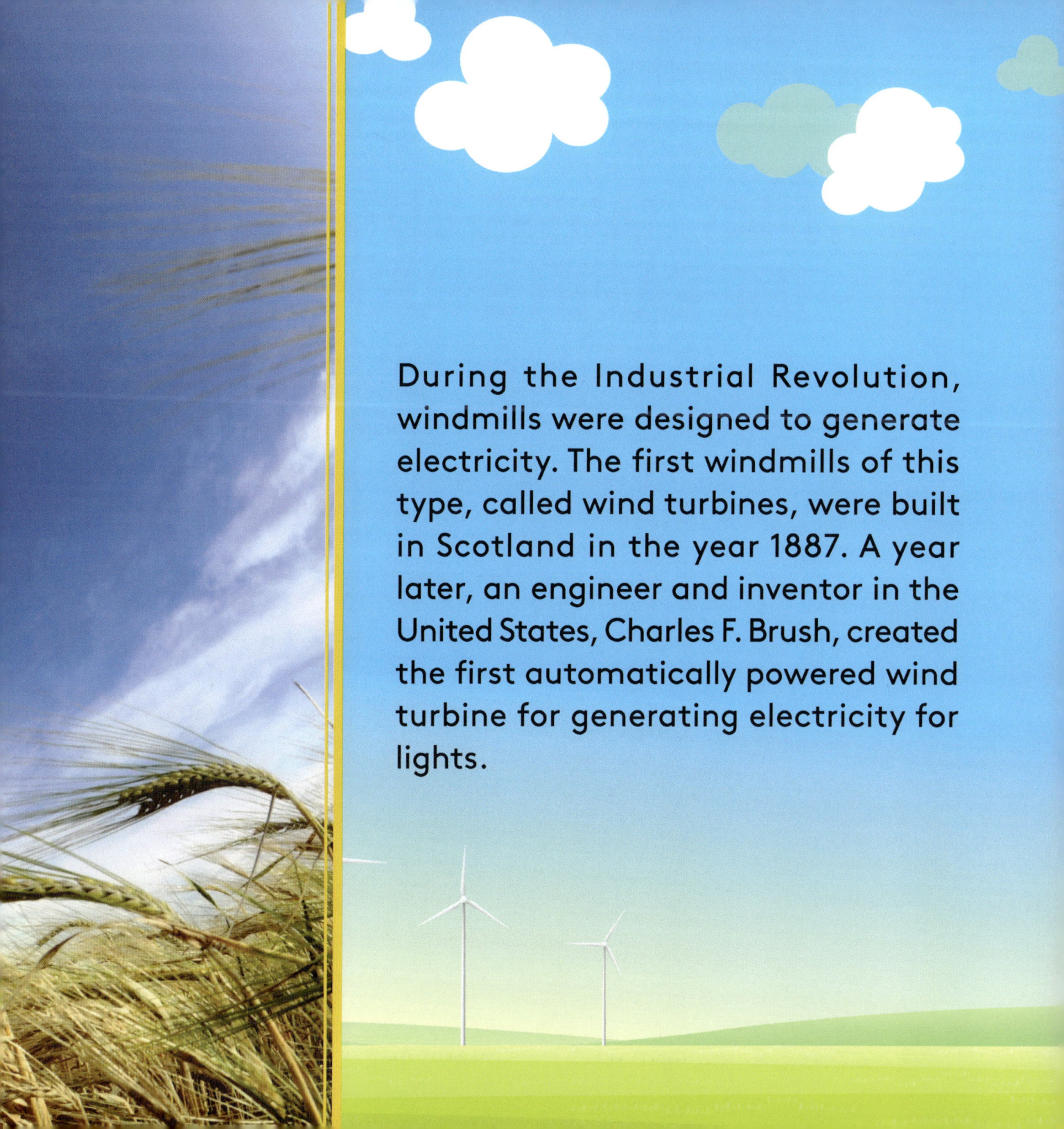

During the Industrial Revolution, windmills were designed to generate electricity. The first windmills of this type, called wind turbines, were built in Scotland in the year 1887. A year later, an engineer and inventor in the United States, Charles F. Brush, created the first automatically powered wind turbine for generating electricity for lights.

WHAT CAUSES WINDS ON THE EARTH'S SURFACE?

The warmth from the Sun is what causes winds to blow on the surface of the Earth. This is why power from the wind is a renewable source of energy because as long as the Sun continues to warm the Earth, there will be sources of wind.

When the Sun rises, the atmosphere over the land warms up more quickly than the atmosphere over the surfaces of water. The hot air is lighter than the cooler air so it rises and the cooler air takes its place. At nighttime, the exact opposite happens.

By this time, the atmosphere over the surfaces of water is warmer. It rises and the cooler land air takes its position. This process, called convection, is what causes the currents of air that we know as wind.

The energy of the moving wind can be transformed into electrical energy through the use of wind turbines.

WHAT IS WIND POWER?

Today, power from the wind is used to turn turbines that generate electricity. The modern designs of these wind turbines are very sleek and well-engineered compared to earlier designs. Wind power is considered to be a very important renewable energy source.

Since there is always wind occurring on the Earth's surface using wind doesn't deplete it as a resource. For the most part, wind turbines don't create any pollution. Because of these advantages, wind turbines are one of the fastest growing types of renewable energy.

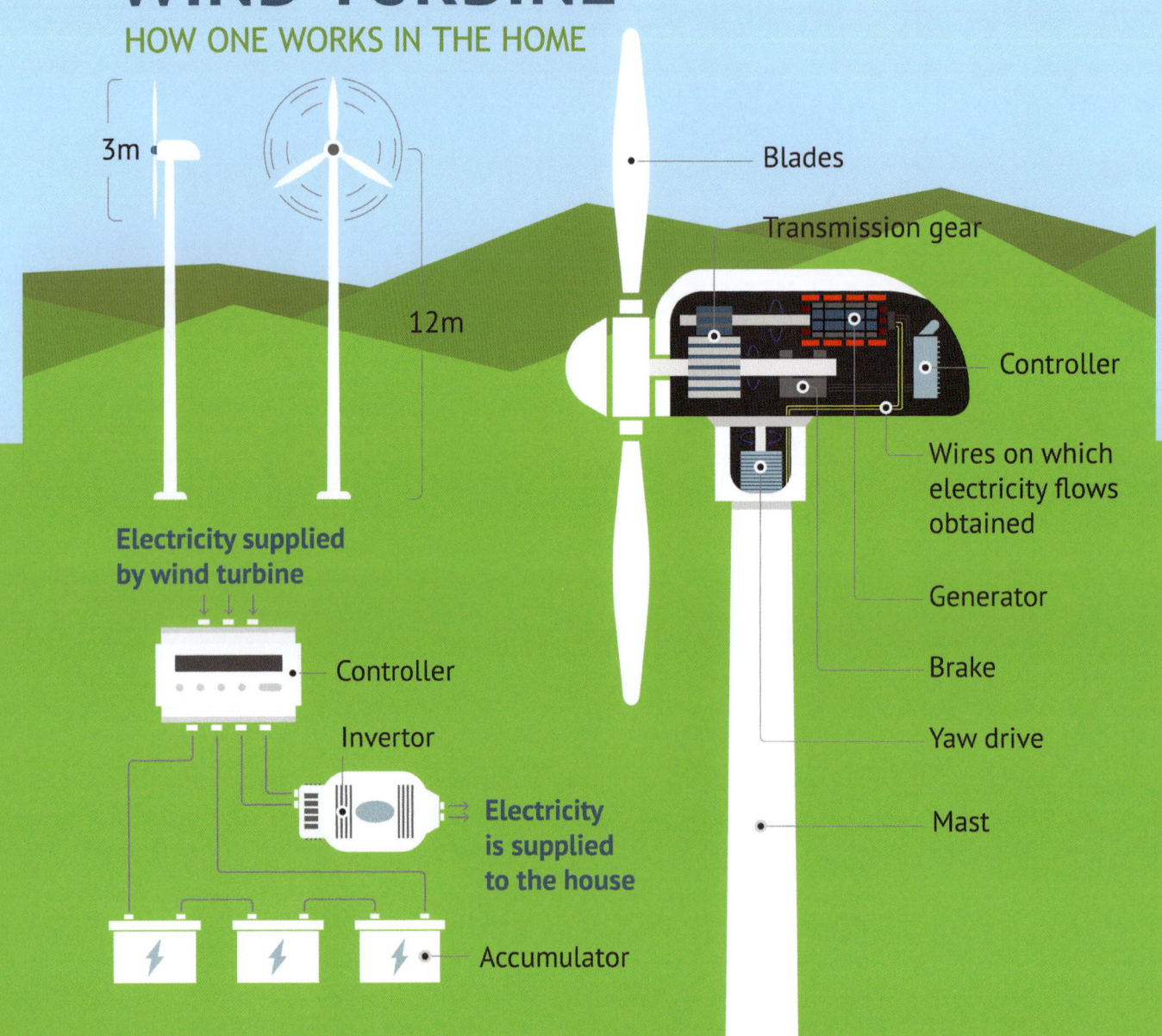

HOW DOES A WIND TURBINE WORK?

If you have a fan at home, you'll notice that when you turn on the electricity the blades of the fan turn to give you air circulation. A wind turbine works in the exact opposite way that a fan does. The wind powers the blades of the wind turbine.

In turn, these moving blades turn a large shaft. Because the shaft is large, it doesn't move fast. However, the gears that are attached to the main shaft power a smaller shaft that turns much more quickly. It's this smaller shaft that is attached to the generator. The generator converts the energy into electricity. Once the electricity is generated, it's sent through transmission lines to a central substation where it is distributed for use in peoples' homes as well as in schools and businesses.

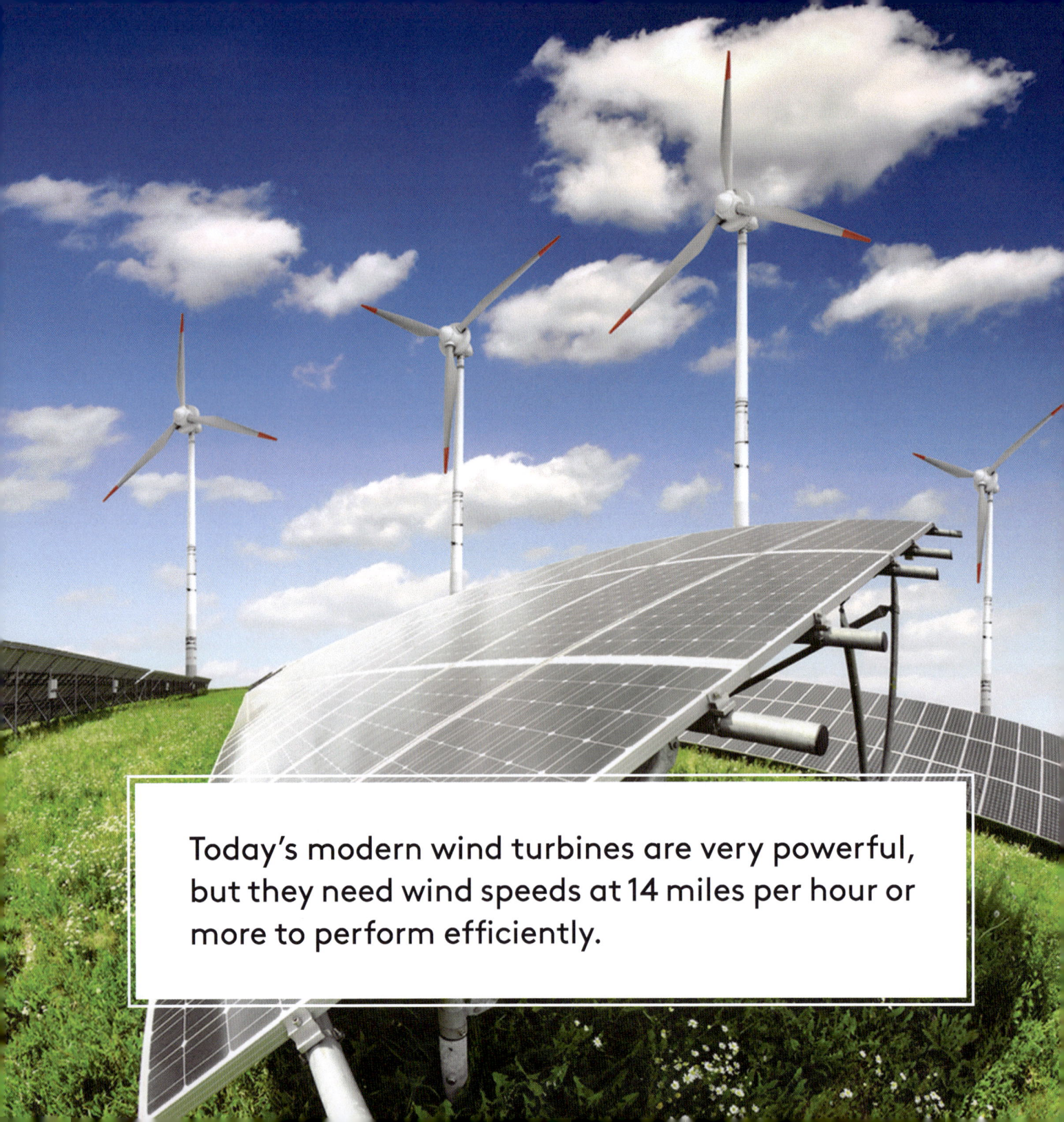

Today's modern wind turbines are very powerful, but they need wind speeds at 14 miles per hour or more to perform efficiently.

One wind turbine working at optimal capacity could generate enough electrical power to give energy to 300 households in a year.

HOW TALL IS A WIND TURBINE?

Today's wind turbines are very tall, much taller than most of the windmills in previous centuries. The towers they are attached to are generally 200 to 300 feet in height.

A PHOTO SHOWING THE TRADITIONAL WINDMILL AND MODERN TURBINE.

If you add in the height of the turbine's blades, the total height is usually at least 400 feet, which is almost as tall as the Great Pyramid in Giza! The blades on the wind turbine are sizable as well. They are usually at least 115 feet in length and some are as long as 148 feet or more. Most wind turbines have three blades.

WHAT IS A WIND FARM?

If you've ever gone for a long drive on highways in the United States, you've probably seen tall, white, wind turbines before. Sometimes there are a few isolated turbines, but you may have come across a huge wind farm that has many turbines.

Energy companies own these large locations with wind turbines and they are called "wind farms." Some wind farms are built in ocean locations and are described as offshore wind farms.

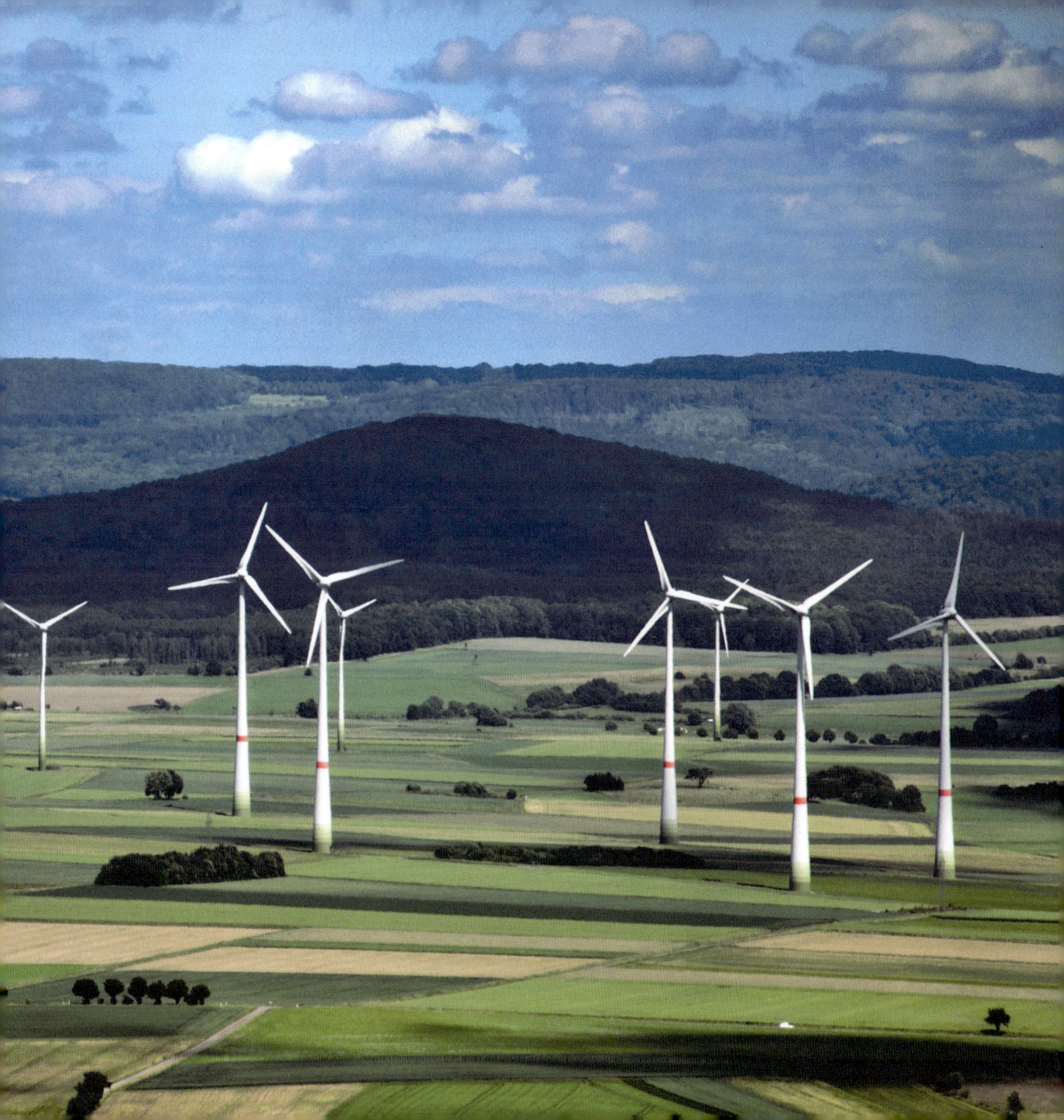

WEST HILLS WIND FARM, WESTERN AUSTRALIA

WHAT HAPPENS IF THERE ISN'T ANY WIND?

If there isn't any wind blowing, then wind turbines can't turn and generate power. However, before a wind farm is constructed, the engineers responsible for building the wind farm will take many measurements in the location being considered.

They will perform the needed research to ensure that the investment the energy company is making in a particular location will return a profit. No matter which location they eventually select, the wind won't blow continuously.

The average wind speed throughout the year and how often the wind blows at that speed are more important than whether the wind is blowing every day.

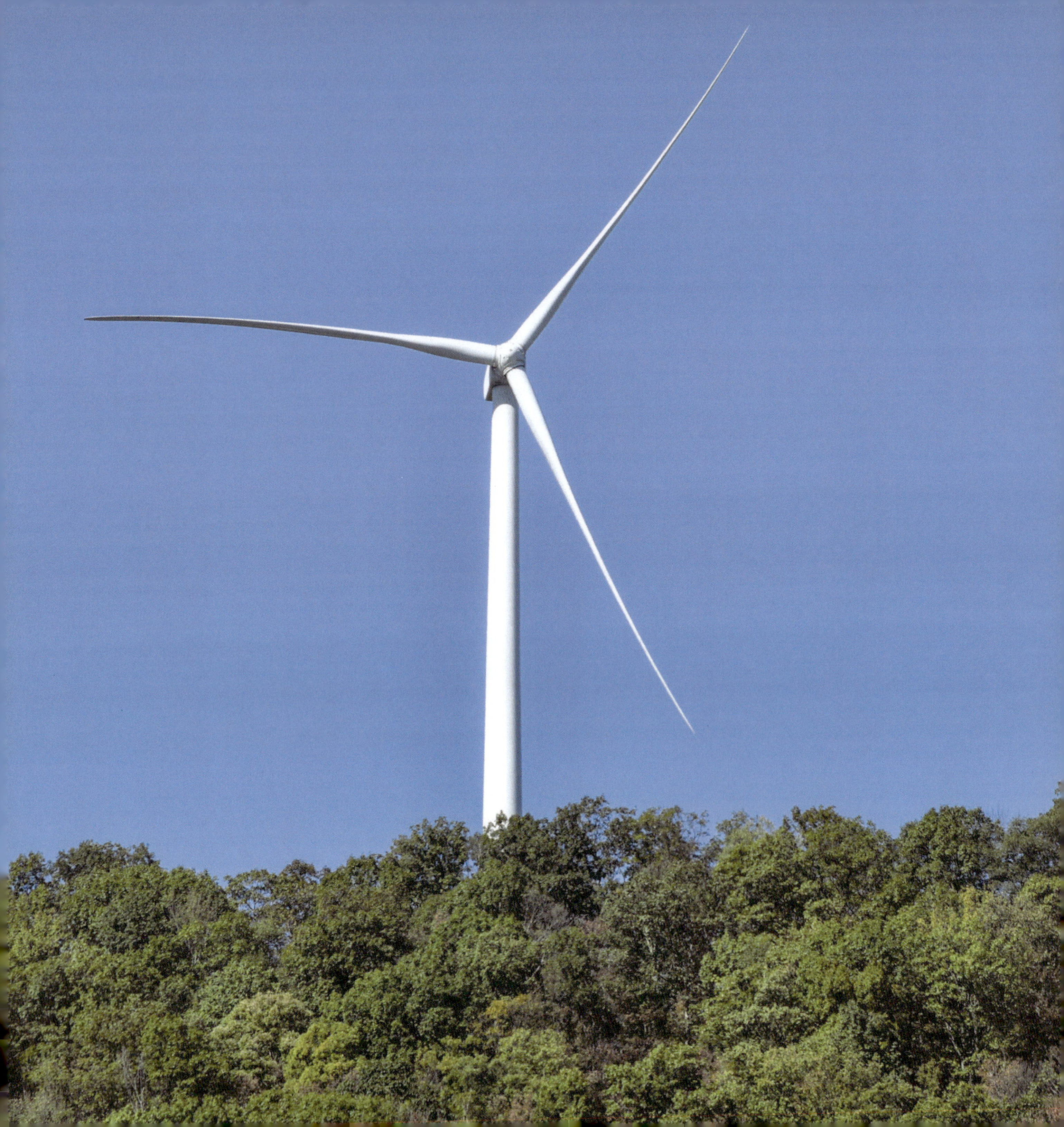

ARE THERE ANY DISADVANTAGES TO WIND POWER?

As with every source of energy, there are some disadvantages to wind power.

Some people dislike the way wind farms look. Because the wind turbines are so large, they tend to destroy some scenic views in hilly areas.

Another drawback is that the wind turbines do make noise, so people who live near them are sometimes disturbed by the "noise pollution" they generate.

One of the largest disadvantages is that birds are sometimes killed by the large blades of the turbines. Engineers are continuously seeking new ways to refine the designs of wind turbines and wind farms to minimize these issues.

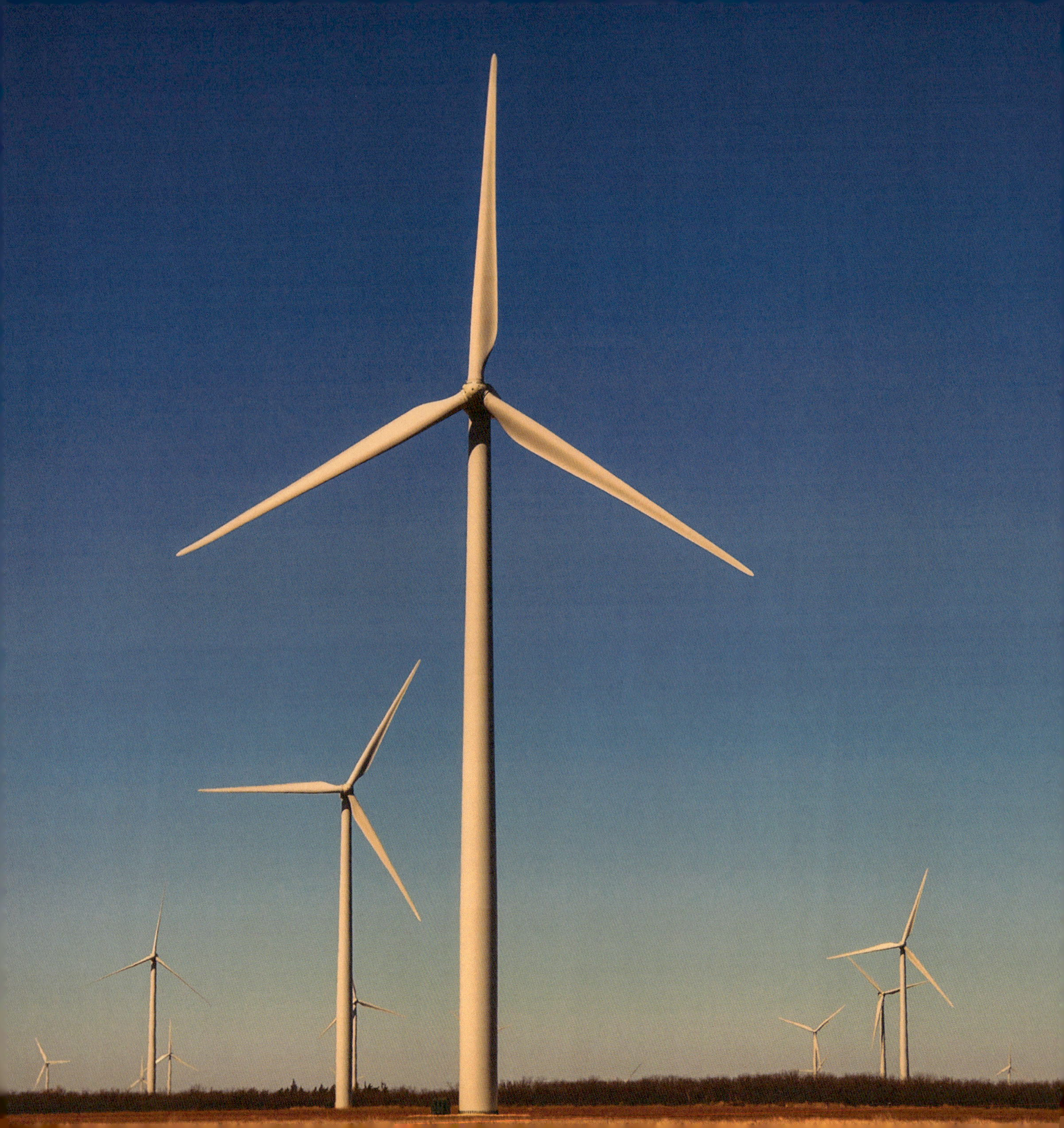

INTERESTING FACTS ABOUT WIND POWER

Texas was the top state for the production of wind power in 2011, followed by the state of Iowa and then California.

There needs to be an average wind speed of 15 mph annually for a wind turbine to return a profit on the energy company's investment.

In 2011, about 3% of all the electricity generated in the US was created by the power of wind. This was enough electricity to service about 10,000,000

residences. By 2016, wind power had increased to 5.5% of the entire power grid.

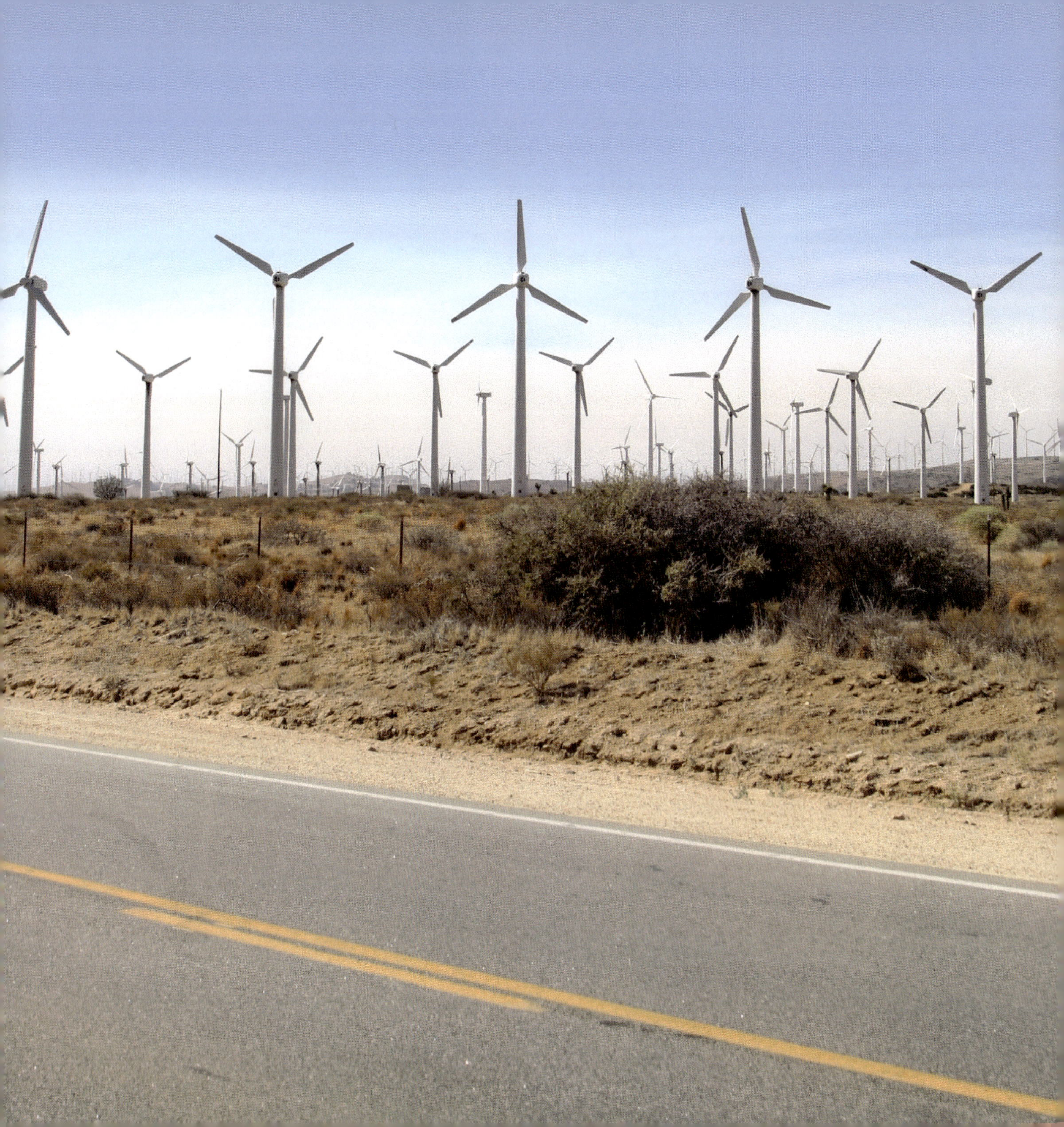

Over the last decade, wind power has grown as a source of energy in the United States due to tax breaks by the government and advances in technology.

One of the largest wind farms in the United States, Horse Hollow, has over 400 wind turbines.

Countries in Europe tend to use wind power more often than other countries around the world because their climate is so windy.

Prairies are great places to set up wind farms because they have wind almost constantly.

China, the United States, and Germany are the top countries for the production of wind-generated electricity worldwide.

CHINA NANTONG COASTAL WIND FARMS

At the end of 2012, there were over 220,000 wind turbines spinning all around the world.

The Gansu Wind Farm in a desert area of China has over 7,000 wind turbines. By the year 2020, the

Chinese government plans to spend about $360 billion on renewable energy sources.

In 2016, there were more than 100,000 jobs in the United States devoted to wind energy. By 2050, it's estimated that over 600,000 jobs in the United States will be related to wind energy.

THE WIND AND ITS POWER

As long as the Sun keeps shining and bringing warmth to the Earth, wind will be created. The warmth of the Sun heats the land and the water differently during the day and at night. This causes a process of convection, which generates the movement of the wind. Wind is a renewable energy source. Although it does have some disadvantages, most people feel that its advantages make it an important energy source that is positioned for growth in the future.

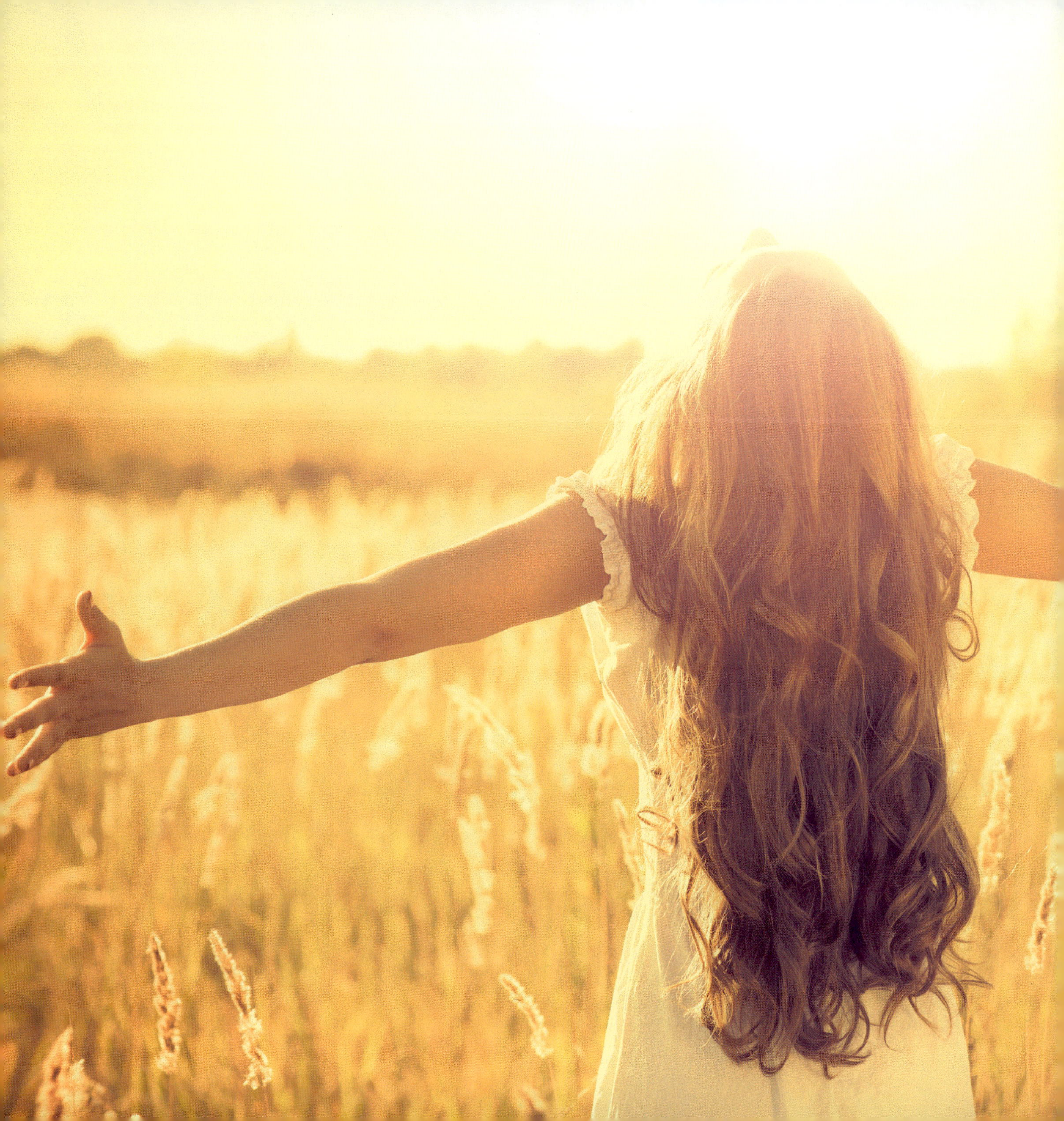

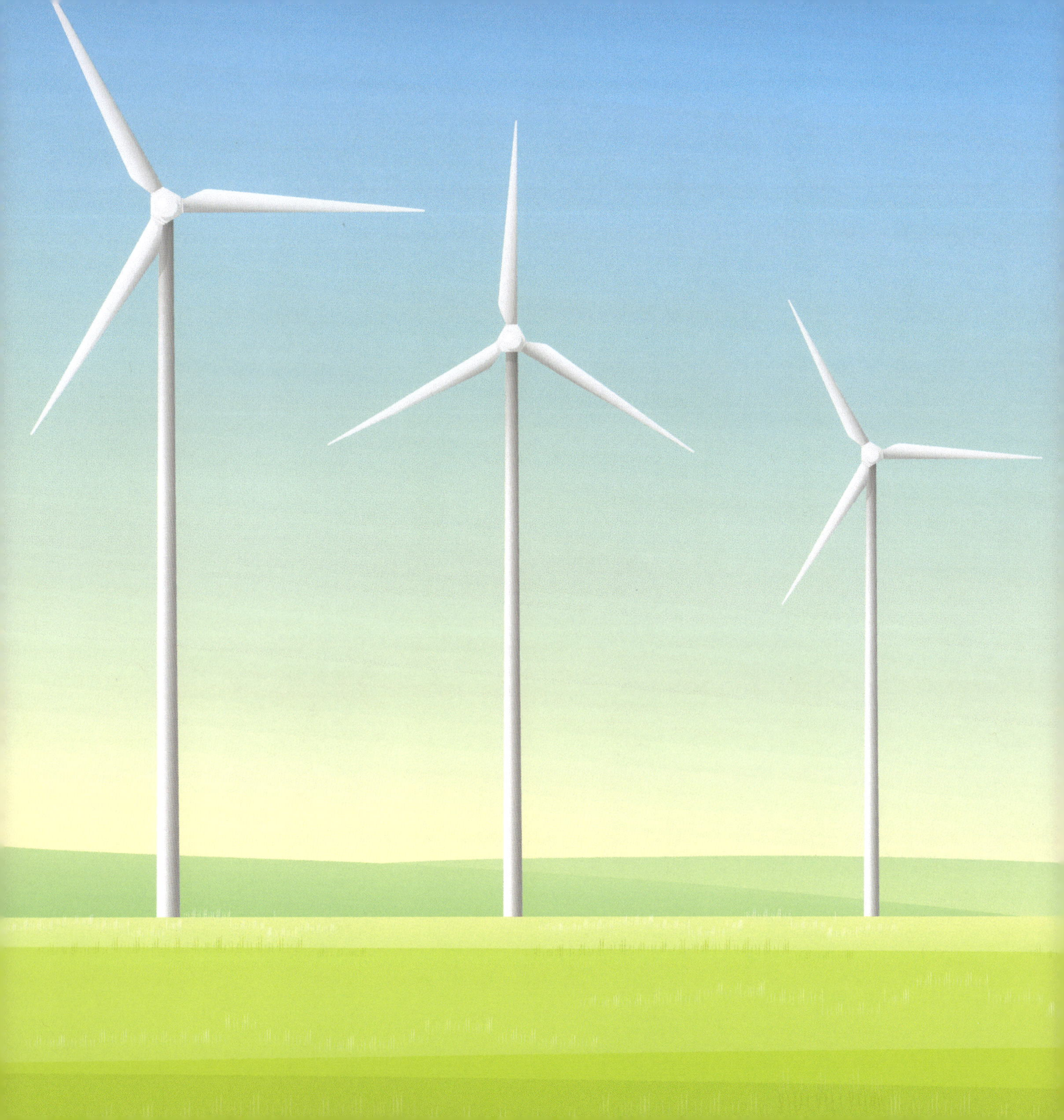

Now that you've read about wind power, you may want to read about other renewable energy sources in the Baby Professor book **Renewable Energy Sources - Wave, Geothermal and Biomass Energy Edition: Environment Books for Kids | Children's Environment Books.**

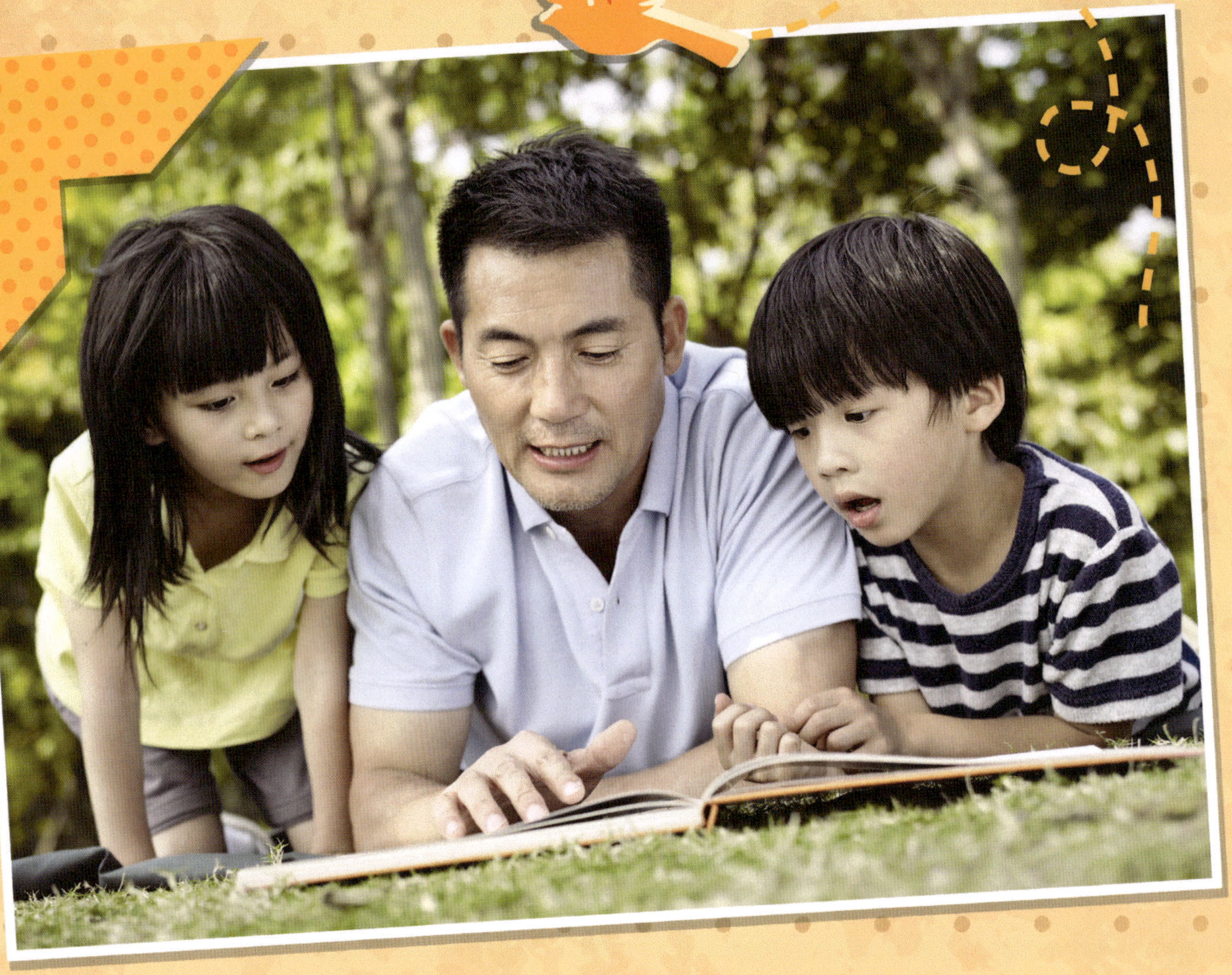

Visit

BABY PROFESSOR
EDUCATION KIDS

www.BabyProfessorBooks.com

to download Free Baby Professor eBooks and view our catalog of new and exciting Children's Books

Printed in Great Britain
by Amazon